Say It With
Color!

Writer's Toolbox of Alternate Color Name

Saves Time, Provides Inspiration for:

Copywriters evoking persuasive visual images

Marketers describing a hot new product

Article writers adding zing to their work

Fundraisers bringing to life a heart-warming story

Bloggers giving vividness to their posts

Web content writers seeking sleek, riveting prose

Novelists and **poets** depicting a blazing winter sunset or the color of love

Anyone who needs a gripping color description not limited to plain "red" or "blue" or "green".

A writer's resource of just about every color you can imagine – all at your fingertips right here.

Hamilton House, 630 County Road 14
RR3 Demorestville, Ontario, Canada K0K 1W0

ISBN 978-0-9811689-9-9

TABLE OF CONTENTS

What Color Can Do For You

Writing, no matter what kind, must appeal to the reader's imagination. Nothing does that better than painting pictures for the mind.

To paint a picture, you must use color!

Color is communication at it's vibrant best. It evokes memory and creates a connection to the mental image.

At a subconscious level, color creates an immediate physiological effect. It can calm, soothe, reassure and lower the pulse rate. Or it can stimulate, excite and send blood racing through the veins. It makes your writing alive and immediate, physically and mentally.

Whether you're a novelist, a poet, a direct mail copywriter, an entrepreneur striving for effective advertising or a lover writing to your sweetheart, color is a powerful tool to get your message across.

Whether on the page or out in the real world, color has a direct impact.

Color Saves a Business

Owners of a new restaurant, for example, wondered why their customers ordered little and refused to linger.

The business was slowly failing – until the owners realized the sleek ice blue decor, combined with the wintery landscape outside, was making their patrons feel chilly and uncomfortable.

 Once redecorated in warm yellow, red and peach tones, the restaurant began to boom as customers suddenly found their appetites and stayed for dessert in the cheery, stimulating atmosphere.

Cool colors – blue, green, silver, turquoise – calm, soothe and recede before the eyes.

Warm colors – red, yellow, orange, pink, gold – stimulate, excite and seem to advance. Choose the right colors and you control the reaction.

The smart writer and the smart entrepreneur know colors can do wonders for business – and for your life.

Colors is one small section of the **Marketing Phrase Book**. Check out this trove of instant, ready-to-use marketing phrases at: www.hamilhouse.com

AUTUMN

The rusts and rich bronzes of autumn bring a feeling of maturity, abundant harvest, wealth and warmth.

AUTUMN

- Amber
- Apricot
- Auburn
- Autumn leaf
- Bay
- Beech
- Brandy
- Brass
- Brandywine
- Brass
- Brick
- Bronze
- Cantaloupe
- Chestnut
- Cider
- Cognac
- Copper
- Copperplate
- Dead leaf
- Desert fox
- Dried Blood
- Ember
- Fall maple
- Ferruginous
- Flower pot
- Fox
- Fox sparrow
- Fire
- Ginger
- Hazel
- Henna
- Irish setter
- Maple
- Marigold
- Marmalade
- Nut
- Ochre
- Old blood
- Pinot noir
- Prairie sunset
- Pumpkin
- Red cedar
- Redwood
- Roan
- Roast Chestnut
- Rosewood
- Ruddy
- Rum

- Russet
- Rust
- Sandstone
- Sorrel
- Spice
- Squash
- Sunset
- Tawny
- Terra cotta
- Tiger eye
- Titian
- Toast
- Tuscan sun
- Vixen
- Whiskey
- Yam

BEIGE

Beige is the truly flexible color, highlighting and absorbing the attributes of whatever is near. It is a traditional relaxing background color. Its neutrality can be seen either as warm or even dull. It is dependable, conservative and a safe choice. Yet it can be a magnificent backdrop to the most daring, brilliant displays.

BEIGE

- Acorn
- Almond
- Alpaca
- Antelope
- Atoll
- Bamboo
- Bare
- Bark
- Basket
- Beach
- Beachside
- Beige
- Biscotti
- Biscuit
- Bisque
- Bistre
- Blonde
- Bluff
- Bone
- Broom

- Buckskin
- Buckwheat
- Buff
- Buff Orpington
- Burlap
- Buttermilk
- Camel
- Chamois
- Champagne
- Clam chowder
- Coconut
- Corn
- Corn husk
- Corn silk
- Corn stalk
- Cove
- Cream
- Cream soup
- Danish blonde
- Deer belly
- Desert
- Desert rat
- Desert hare
- Dove
- Driftwood
- Dun
- Dusk
- Dust
- Dust storm
- Ecru
- Eggshell
- Fawn
- Flax
- Flaxen
- Grain
- Greige
- Hay
- Honey
- Honeycomb
- Khaki
- Lace
- Latte
- Linen
- Lion
- Lynx
- Maple sugar
- Marsh grass
- Moccasin
- Mojave
- Mushroom
- Natural
- Neutral
- Nude
- Oat
- Oatmeal
- Outback
- Palomino
- Papyrus
- Parchment
- Prairie
- Pear
- Puma

- Raffia
- Rattan
- Rice
- Sable
- Sack
- Safari
- Sand
- Sandblast
- Sandstone
- Sea shell
- Sea grass
- Sesame
- Shell
- Sisal
- Soybean

- Straw
- Suede
- Tan
- Taupe
- Tawny
- Toast
- Viking blond
- Wheat
- Wheaten
- Whole wheat
- Wicker
- Wooden shoe

BLACK

BLACK, the absence of color, is confident, strong, conservative. It has a powerful air of mystery yet can be sexy and sophisticated, providing a vivid contrast to whatever is juxtaposed. Black can also mean mourning, sorrow and evil.

Phrases: black box, black tie, black belt, in the black, pitch black, black hat, black sheep, black market, blackguard, black-hearted, blacklist, blackmail, black eye, black out, black and blue, blackball, black books

BLACK

- Andiron
- Anvil
- Asphalt
- Basalt
- Bear paw
- Beetle
- Bile
- Bird's eye
- Bitumen
- Black
- Black bean
- Black bear
- Black fly
- Black tie
- Black ice
- Black cat
- Black current
- Blackberry
- Blackout
- Blasted
- Bolt
- Bull
- Bunker oil
- Burnt
- Cannon
- Cave
- Char
- Charcoal
- Chimney
- Chimney sweep
- Cinder
- Cinderblock
- Clinker
- Cinder
- Coal
- Coroner
- Crow
- Crude oil
- Demon
- Devil's
- Ebony
- Exhaust
- Fire pit
- Frostbite
- Funeral
- Funereal
- Gangrene
- Grave bottom
- Graveyard
- Grease
- Hades
- Hell
- Highway
- India ink
- Ink
- Iron
- Jet
- Killer whale
- Lampblack
- Loam

- Midnight
- Mine
- Moonless
- Mourner
- Mourning cloak
- Murky
- Nightmare
- Nuclear winter
- Obsidian
- Oil patch
- Oil
- Oil spill
- Old rubber
- Onyx
- Panther
- Patent leather
- Penguin
- Pepper
- Persian lamb
- Pit
- Raisin
- Raven
- Rot
- Sable
- Shadow
- Shoe polish
- Silhouette
- Sin
- Skunk
- Sludge
- Smoke
- Soot
- Spanish bull
- Spider
- Styx
- Swart
- Tarmac
- Thunderhead
- Toro
- Tractor tire
- Transmission oil
- Truffle
- Tunnel
- Underworld
- Whale back

BLUE

BLUE calms the mind, lowers blood pressure and decreases respiration. It is the color of the sky. It is strong, steadfast and trustworthy. It is associated with confidence, stability, importance and conservatism. Note how many banks and corporations choose blue as their color. Many services, such as police and security officers wear blue uniforms as a sign of reassurance. Seen as a source of peace, blue is great for bedrooms as it is conducive to sleep.

Phrases: true blue, out of the blue, wild blue yonder, blue skies, blue skying, blue ribbon, blue Monday, blue blood, baby blue, got the blues, blue heaven, deep blue sea, blue horizon, the blues, post-partum blues, into the blue, swear a blue streak, blue nose, blue Monday, blue note, singing the blues, blue with cold, blue collar, blue pencil, blue-eyed, blue ribbon, blue in the face, boys in blue, feeling blur

TURQUOISE
TURQUOISE is calming and sophisticated. It is the refreshing color of water and tropical bays. It is a wonderful rich blue stone speaking of the American Southwest.

BLUE

- Adriatic
- Admiral
- Aegean
- Alice
- Aqua
- Aquamarine
- Arctic
- Azure
- Baby
- Bayou
- Berry
- Beryl

13

- Blowfly
- Blue mould
- Blue spruce
- Blueberry
- Bluebird
- Blue jay
- Bruise
- Capri
- Cascade
- Cedar berry
- Cerulean
- Cesious
- Chalybeous
- Chevy
- Cobalt
- Cornflower
- Cote D'Azur
- Cyan
- Cyaneous
- Dagger
- Deepwater
- Deep sea
- Denim
- Flag
- Forget-me-not
- Gentian
- Great Lake
- Harbour
- Harebell
- Heron
- Horizon
- Iceberg
- Ice blue
- Indigo
- Iris
- Lake
- Lapis lazuli
- Loyal
- Loyalist
- Lupin
- Marine
- Mazarine
- Midnight
- Morning glory
- Mountain pool
- Navy
- Nile
- Ocean
- Pacific
- Patriot
- Peacock
- Periwinkle
- Planet
- Police
- Pool
- Poolside
- Porcelain
- Powder
- Prussian
- Regatta
- Robin's egg
- Royal

- Sapphire
- Sea
- Seacrest
- Seaside
- Slate
- Sky
- Spode
- Spruce
- Steel
- Submarine
- Teal
- Tory
- Tranquility
- Tropic
- True
- Turquoise
- Ultramarine
- Wedgewood
- Whirlpool
- Wildflower
- Woad

BROWN

BROWN is earthiness, dependability, solid grounding and steadfastness. It is friends and warmth, representing the very earth beneath our feet. It also can be chosen by corporations wanting to project stability.

Phrases: brown bag, brown out, brown study, brown off, brown nose, browner

BROWN

- Acorn
- Adobe
- Ale
- Allspice
- Almond
- Alpaca
- Anchovy
- Appleseed
- Armadillo
- Auburn
- Augean
- Bannock
- Bark
- Barley

- Barn owl
- Barracuda
- Barrel
- Bay
- Bayou
- Beagle
- Beaver
- Beech
- Beer
- Beetle
- Biscuit
- Bisque
- Boa Constrictor
- Boardwalk
- Bog
- Boredom
- Bouillon
- Bovril
- Bracken
- Brandy
- Briar
- Bridle
- Bronze
- Broth
- Brown sugar
- Brown bag
- Brunette
- Buckskin
- Bunny
- Burlap
- Burnt umber
- Burnt sienna
- Caffeine
- Calfskin
- Cappuccino
- Caramel
- Cardboard
- Carob
- Cedar
- Chestnut
- Chimpanzee
- Chocolate
- Cider
- Cinnabar
- Cinnamon
- Cinnamon stick
- Cinnespice
- Clove
- Cockroach
- Cocoa
- Cocoa bean
- Coconut
- Codfish
- Coffee grounds
- Coffee
- Coffin
- Cognac
- Cookie
- Copper
- Copper mine
- Corduroy
- Cordwood

- Cork
- Cowhide
- Coyote
- Crocodile
- Cumin
- Dapple
- Dead leaf
- Dirt road
- Dune
- Eagle
- Earth
- Earthwood
- Earwig
- Ecru
- English saddle
- Espresso
- Falcon
- Fava
- Fawn
- French toast
- French roast
- Fresh bread
- Fruitwood
- Fudge
- Ginger
- Gingerbread
- Ginger snap
- Gopher
- Grizzly
- Guitar
- Hazel
- Hedgehog
- Heartwood
- Hickory
- Honey
- Honey mead
- Hop sack
- Horseback
- Irish whiskey
- Jackrabbit
- Java
- Jersey cow
- Jute
- Khaki
- Leather
- Liver
- Macaroon
- Mahogany
- Mainsail
- Maple
- Maple syrup
- Mincemeat
- Mink
- Moccasin
- Mocha
- Mongrel
- Monkey
- Moose
- Mud
- Mud slide
- Muddy water
- Muskrat

- Mussel
- Mustang
- Nut
- Oak
- Ochre
- Oil
- Old spice
- Otter
- Ox hide
- Peanut
- Peanut butter
- Peat
- Pecan
- Pigskin
- Pine cone
- Pine needle
- Porcupine
- Potato
- Prairie dog
- Puce
- Quail
- Raisin
- Rattlesnake
- Rawhide
- Redwood
- Reindeer
- Roach
- Russet
- Sand
- Sandstorm
- Sable
- Saddle
- Sandalwood
- Seal
- Sienna
- Sepia
- Sherry
- Shipping crate
- Shoe leather
- Sienna
- Sisal
- Silt
- Snakeskin
- Snuff
- Spice
- Stoat
- Stout
- Stucco
- Sugar shack
- Syrup
- Tabby
- Tadpole
- Taffy
- Tan
- Tanbark
- Tawny
- Tea leaves
- Tea
- Tea Stain
- Teak
- Terra cotta
- Thatch

- Timber
- Toast
- Tobacco
- Toffee
- Truffle
- Tweed
- Twig
- Umber
- Vandyke
- Walnut
- Whiskey
- Wood

CLEAR

CLEAR is there and not there. It is the lens that lets us look through to what is behind.

CLEAR

- Angel tear
- Acquavite
- Cloudless
- Colorless
- Crystal
- Crystalline
- Diamond
- Diaphanous
- Ethereal
- Glassy
- Ice
- Ice cube
- Invisible
- Lambent
- Lacquer
- Lens
- Limpid
- Look through
- Lucid
- Mountain air
- Mirror
- Naked
- Pellucid
- Plexiglas
- Pure
- Pure soul
- Raindrop
- Sparkler
- Stainless
- Star
- Starlight
- Teardrop

- Telescope
- Transparent
- Translucent
- Uncolored

- Unseen
- Vermouth
- Vodka
- Water

GENERAL

GENERAL can include all sorts and kinds of things

- Balloon
- Bird of paradise
- Calliope
- Chevy
- Fiesta
- Hollyhock
- Horizon
- Iridescent
- Jujube

- Lollipop
- Neon brights
- Nordic
- Notice-me
- Pale
- Pastels
- Primaries
- Rainbow
- Two-tone

GREEN

GREEN is the color of nature and life. It signifies growth, health, abundance, renewal, one with nature, spring, Ireland, environmental responsibility. It soothes relaxes both mentally and physically. It gives the fresh feeling of summer. Olive green can have a military feel. Green can also signify jealousy, envy, greed, inexperience, illness and decay.

Phrases: green thumb, greener pastures, going green, greenback, green-eyed with jealousy, green-eyed monster, green with envy, green with age, green about the gills, greenhorn, green wash, green bash, green belt

GREEN

- Absinthe
- Acacia
- Acid
- Alfalfa
- Alfresco
- Algae
- Alligator
- Aloe
- Aloe vera
- Alpine
- Amazon
- Amphibian
- Anise
- Aphid
- Apple
- April
- Army
- Artichoke
- Asparagus
- Atoll
- Avocado
- Bamboo
- Basil
- Beach grass
- Bosky
- Bottle
- Boxwood
- Broccoli
- Bullfrog
- Cabbage
- Camouflage
- Catnip
- Celedone
- Celery
- Chartreuse
- Chlorophyll
- Clover
- Crocodile
- Cucumber
- Cypress
- Dill pickle
- Dinosaur
- Emerald
- English garden
- Eucalyptus
- Fern
- Foliage
- Forest
- Forest ranger
- Forrester

- Frog
- Garden
- Garden hose
- Grass
- Grinch
- Guacamole
- Hazel
- Hemlock
- Holly
- Honeydew melon
- Hunter
- Huntsman
- Iguana
- Irish
- Ivy
- Jack pine
- Jade
- Jungle fever
- Jungle
- Juniper
- Kale
- Kelly
- Kelp
- Key lime
- Khaki
- Kiwi
- Laurel
- Leaf
- Leapfrog
- Leek
- Lentil
- Leopard frog
- Leprechaun
- Lettuce
- Lichen
- Lily pad
- Lime
- Limeade
- Limeade
- Linden
- Lizard
- Malachite
- Mantis
- Marsh
- Meadow
- Mermaid
- Mint
- Mistletoe
- Mould
- Moss
- Myrtle
- Nettle
- Olive
- Olive oil
- Orchard
- Parakeet
- Parsley
- Pea
- Pea pod
- Pear
- Peat moss
- Pesto

- Philodendron
- Pickle
- Pine
- Pistachio
- Plantain
- Pond scum
- Primavera
- Puke
- Putting green
- Ragweed
- Rainforest
- Raw
- Relish
- Romaine
- Sage
- Sagebrush
- Salad
- Sap
- Sapling
- Sassafras
- Scotch pine
- Sea grass
- Sea
- Seafoam
- Seasick
- Seaweed
- Secret Garden
- Sequoia
- Shamrock
- Sherwood
- Snow pea
- Spinach
- Sporting
- Spring
- Spring wheat
- Sprout
- Spruce
- Surf
- Swamp
- Swamp water
- Tea
- Tea tree
- Tree
- Tree house
- Treetop
- Traffic light
- Turtle
- Unripe
- Verdant
- Vertigo
- Vomit
- Verdant
- Verdurous
- Verdure
- Watermelon
- Weed
- Weeping willow
- Willow
- Wintergreen
- Wolf
- Yew
- Yucca

GREY

GREY is cool and conservative, elegant and quietly neutral. It can denote a mood of sadness or mourning, yet it is also the color of clouds and mist and stormy waters. Grey is a way to blend in without show and suggest quiet contemplation.

Phrases: Grey power, grey matter, grey water, grey days, greyed out, grey area, grey zone, going grey, grey eminence

SILVER

Cool, sleek, elegant, shining, metallic, rich, this gleaming precious metal is a natural counterpoint to the richness and warmth of gold.

Phrases: silver-tongued, silver screen, silver-haired, silver bullet, silver lining, silver spoon, silver-voiced

GREY

- Abbey
- Accomplice
- Adulterer
- Aluminium
- Ambush
- Amnesia
- Anchor
- Ash
- Ashen
- Bailiff
- Bark
- Barn board
- Barn wall
- Barnacle
- Barred rock
- Battle
- Battleship
- Bilge water
- Bistre
- Brain
- Burnt Silver

24

- Castle
- Cement
- Chalice
- Chanterelle
- Charcoal
- Chrome
- Chromium
- Cinder
- Cinereal
- Clay
- Cloud
- Cobblestone
- Coin
- Concrete
- Dawn
- Dead Sea
- Deadwood
- Death
- Death Valley
- Depression
- Dingy
- Dishwater
- Dolphin
- Dove
- Dovecote
- Drab
- Driftwood
- Drizzle
- Dusk
- Dust
- Elephant
- Flint
- Fog
- Fossil
- Galvanized
- German silver
- Glaucous
- Granite
- Graphite
- Gravel
- Greige
- Greystone
- Grime
- Grit
- Gunmetal
- Gunpowder
- Haggis
- Hail
- Hailstorm
- Haze
- Hearthstone
- Heather
- Highway
- Hippopotamus
- Hurricane
- Iceberg
- Iron
- Iron ore
- Jailor
- Lard
- Lead
- Lichen

- Limestone
- Livid
- Mercury
- Militia
- Mist
- Mole
- Moonbeam
- Moonstone
- Mold
- Mouse
- Mushroom
- Nacreous
- Nickel
- Night mist
- Nimbus
- Old barn/house
- Overcast
- Oyster
- Payne's
- Pearl
- Pebble
- Pewter
- Porpoise
- Porridge
- Powder
- Prison
- Pudding
- Putty
- Rhino
- Sea
- Seal
- Sere
- Shadow
- Shale
- Sharkskin
- Sheet metal
- Silver
- Silver fox
- Silverbright
- Slate
- Sludge
- Smoke
- Smoky glass
- Smudge
- Somber
- Stainless steel
- Steamship
- Steel
- Sterling
- Stingray
- Storm cloud
- Stone
- Stone age
- Stone fish
- Stone wall
- Storm
- Storm cloud
- Taupe
- Toad
- Toadstool
- Tornado
- Tuna

- Twilight
- Walrus
- Weathered
- Whale
- Wharf
- Whetstone
- Zinc

JEWEL

JEWELS evoke sparkle, glitter, beauty, glamour, dazzle, romance, wealth, mystery, danger and desire.

JEWEL

- Agate
- Amber
- Aquamarine
- Beryl
- Bloodstone
- Carnelian
- Chalcedony
- Chrysoberyl
- Coral
- Crystal
- Citrine
- Diamond
- Emerald
- Fire opal
- Garnet
- Jade
- Labradorite
- Lapis lazuli
- Malachite
- Moonstone
- Onyx
- Opal
- Pearl
- Peridot
- Quartz
- Rhinestone
- Rose quartz
- Ruby
- Sapphire
- Sardonyx
- Spinel
- Sunstone
- Topaz
- Tourmaline
- Turquoise
- Zircon

METAL

METALS are strong, hard, shining, protective or dangerous and can bring prosperity or greed.

Phrases: golden girl/boy, golden handshake, gold standard, sounding brass, lead overshoes, steely-eyes, tin horn, iron clad, sterling character, silver-tongued

METAL

- Aluminum
- Bronze
- Chrome
- Copper
- Gold
- Gun metal
- Iron
- Lead
- Nickel
- Platinum
- Silver
- Stainless steel
- Steel
- Tin
- Titanium
- Tungsten
- Zinc

MIXED

MIXED for all the wonderful and infinite variety of colors and shades in our vast and varied world.

Phrases: mixed blessing, mixed up, mix and match, into the mix, part of the mix, mix it up, pick and mix

MIXED

- Agate
- Appaloosa
- Banded
- Barred

- Blaze
- Blend
- Brindled
- Butterfly
- Calico
- Cat's whisker
- Chequered
- Cosmic
- Dapple
- Dotted
- Easter egg
- Flecked
- Freckle
- Gingham
- Harlequin
- Hazel
- Kaleidoscope
- Leopard
- Magpie
- Marble
- Masquerade
- Mongrel
- Mosaic
- Motley
- Mottle
- Multicolored
- Multihued
- Neopolitan
- Oil slick
- Opal
- Panda
- Particolored
- Paint
- Painted brick
- Patchwork
- Penguin
- Pepper and salt
- Pied
- Piebald
- Pinto
- Plaid
- Polychrome
- Potpourri
- Poxy
- Prism
- Prismatic
- Psychedelic
- Rainbow
- Sale and pepper
- Snake back
- Snake eye
- Specked
- Speckled
- Spotted
- Stained glass
- Streaked
- Striated
- Striped
- Tabby
- Tiger
- Tiger eye
- Tiger tail

- Tortoise shell
- Tweed
- Varied

- Variegated
- Zebra

NEUTRAL

NEUTRAL is to be unnoticed, peaceful, the perfect background. See also **BEIGE.**

NEUTRAL

- Almond
- Bisque
- Bleached
- Bone
- Canvas
- Chamomile
- Clam chowder
- Cougar
- Eggshell
- Freeze
- Greige
- Ironstone
- Jute

- Linen
- Marble
- Morel
- Natural
- New dawn
- Parched
- Parchment
- Powder
- Rice
- Travertine
- Twilight
- Vellum
- Vichyssoise

ORANGE

ORANGE is also a warm, sunny stimulant, giving vibrant energy. It is the brilliant leaves of autumn, the juice of an orange, the glory of a sunset and can mean change. Orange demands attention, and encourages social interaction, yet can mean caution, a signal to beware.

ORANGE

- Apricot
- Bittersweet berry
- Bonfire
- Branding iron
- Brass
- Bronze
- Brush fire
- Cadmium
- Cantaloupe
- Cardinal
- Carrot
- Cat's eye
- Cheddar
- Cheese
- Cider
- Copper
- Coral
- Crayon
- Day lily
- Demon eye
- Devil's tongue
- Ember
- Fire
- Flame
- Forest fire
- Ginger
- Goldfish
- Honey
- Hot coal
- Lava
- Life jacket
- Lipstick
- Mango
- Marigold
- Marmalade
- Marsh fire
- Melon
- Molten
- Nectarine
- Orangeade
- Ochre
- Ochreous

- Orange crush
- Oriole
- Papaya
- Peach
- Persian melon
- Persimmon
- Prairie fire
- Pumpkin
- Russet
- Safety vest
- Salmon
- Sandstone
- Snapdragon
- Solar flare
- Spice
- Squash
- Sundog
- Sunfire
- Sunset
- Sunrise
- Sweet potato
- Tangelo
- Tangerine
- Tiger
- Tiger lily
- Titan
- Traffic light
- Tuscan
- Wildfire
- Yam

PINK

PINK is the softer version of red. It soothes and relaxes and evokes warmth and happiness, sweetness and peace. It is playful, delicate and charming. Too much pink is thought to cause physical weakness. It is associated with romance and it's darker shades can denote strong passion and the political left. It is also said to make us crave sugar.

Phrases: tickled pink, pink collar, in the pink, pink (to notch or rap), pinko, pink cloud, rose (pink) colored glasses, pretty in pink, pink carnation, pink ghetto, pink slip, pinkie finger, pinking shears, pink triangle

PINK

- Abalone
- Acne
- Adonis
- Affronted
- Baby
- Baby's breath
- Baby's bum
- Ballerina
- Ballet slipper
- Bashful
- Bee balm
- Bloom
- Blossom
- Blush
- Bolshevik
- Bolshie
- Bo-peep
- Bougainvillea
- Bubble gum
- Bougainvillea
- Camellia
- Cheerleader
- Communist
- Commie
- Coral
- Crepe
- Dawn
- Daybreak
- Diaper rash
- Embarrassment
- Eraser
- Fever
- Firebird
- Flamingo
- Flesh
- Flush
- Foxglove
- Fuschia
- Geranium
- Grapefruit
- Hickey
- Hot pink
- Infant
- Intestine
- Lemonade
- Lipstick
- Little girl
- Magenta
- Magnolia
- Mallow
- Melon
- Mortification
- Newborn
- Nursery
- Orchid
- Peach
- Peony
- Petunia
- Piglet
- Pill

- Pimple
- Pinkeye
- Pinko
- Primrose
- Punch
- Rash
- Rhapsody
- Rose
- Roseate
- Rose mist
- Rosewood
- Rouge
- Rubicund
- Salmon
- Sea shell
- Shame
- Shell
- Shocking
- Shrimp
- Shy
- Spun
- Spun sugar
- Sugarplum
- Sun kissed
- Sunrise
- Sunset
- Sweet sixteen
- Sweetheart
- Toenail
- Tongue
- Tuna
- Udder
- Watermelon
- Wild rose

PURPLE

PURPLE is a peaceful color, suppressing the appetite, soothing headaches. It is full of mystery and spirituality and encourages creativity. It is a noble color chosen by royalty. Dark purple is associated with mourning and is the color of honor for those distinguished or wounded in battle.

Phrases: purple prose, purple cow, purple speech, royal purple, emperor purple, purple haze

LAVENDER

LAVENDER suggests grace, elegance, refinement and femininity. It is soft, calming color that indicates something special and precious. It is full of nostalgia and romance

PURPLE

- Amethyst
- Amethystine
- Aster
- Aubergine
- Bacchanalian
- Beet
- Bilberry
- Blackberry
- Boysenberry
- Bordeaux
- Bruise
- Burgundy
- Chokeberry
- Chokecherry
- Claret
- Damson
- Eggplant
- Elderberry
- Fuschia
- Garnet
- Grape
- Grappa
- Heather
- Heliotrope
- Hyacinth
- Imperial
- Iris
- Juniper berry
- Lava
- Lavande
- Lavender
- Lilac
- Liver
- Magenta
- Maroon
- Mauve
- Missouri currant
- Morning glory
- Mulberry
- Orchid
- Pansy
- Peony
- Plum
- Pomegranate
- Port
- Puce
- Raisin
- Rowanberry

- Royal
- Sangria
- Sapphire
- Sugarplum

- Thistle
- Violet
- Wine
- Wisteria

RED

RED is a powerful stimulant. It increases brain wave activity, heart rate, respiration and blood pressure. This hot color evokes strong emotion, everything from fiery love to war, anger and battle fever. For much of the world, it means good luck, prosperity and happiness. It also grabs attention and means alarm, danger, stop.

Red signals power. Look how many countries have chosen red for their flags or political movements have chosen red for their color. Think of the red carpet rolled out for very important people.

Phrases: seeing red, red rage, red flag, red zone, code red, red carpet, Red Cross, in the red, red line, red alert, red-handed, red tape, paint the town red, red letter day, red light district, red face, red eye, red-headed, red hot, red herring

RED

- Acne
- Alder
- Alizarin
- Apple
- Bacon
- Barn

- Barn door
- Baroness crimson
- Bashful
- Battle
- Beef
- Beet

- Beetroot
- Berry
- Bleeding
- Blood
- Bloodshot
- Bloodstain
- Bloodstone
- Blush
- Bolshevik
- Borscht
- Brick
- Brickstone
- Bullfighter
- Burn
- Candy
- Candy apple
- Cardinal
- Carmine
- Carnation
- Catsup
- Cerise
- Cherry tree
- Cherry
- Cherries jubilee
- Chinese
- Christmas
- Claret
- Cochineal
- Communist
- Commie
- Corrosion
- Cossack
- Crab apple
- Cranberry
- Crimson
- Crime scene
- Currant
- Demon eye
- Devil
- Diaper rash
- Dried blood
- Embarrassment
- Erubescent
- Ferrari
- Fiesta
- Fireweed
- Flag
- Flame
- Florid
- Fox
- Fury
- Gangrene
- Gardenia
- Garnet
- Geranium
- Grenadier
- Heart throb
- Heart's blood
- Hellfire
- Hereford
- Holly berry
- Hollyhock

- Holiday
- Hot face
- Humiliation
- Imperial scarlet
- Incarnadine
- Indian summer
- Infection
- Inferno
- Inflamed
- Jalapeño
- Jam
- Japanese maple
- Jubilation
- Kirsch
- Knife fight
- Lava
- Lipstick
- Lobster
- Macintosh
- Madder
- Mahogany
- Maraschino
- Moroccan
- Mortal wound
- Mortification
- Mountain ash
- Mountie
- Murder
- Nuclear holocaust
- Ochre
- Ox blood
- Pigeon's blood
- Pimiento
- Pimple
- Poinsettia
- Poppy
- Provocation
- Radish
- Rage
- Rampage
- Rash
- Raspberry
- Raspberry jam
- Raw
- Raw steak
- Redbud
- Red cedar
- Red coat
- Red squirrel
- Redwood
- Revolution
- Rhode Island
- Rhubarb
- Roof tile
- Rooster
- Rose hip
- Rosewood
- Rouge
- Rubicund
- Ruby
- Ruddy
- Russian

- Salamander
- Sanguine
- Santa
- Scarlet
- Scald
- Scarlet fever
- Scarlet oak
- Sear
- Showstopper
- Siren
- Slash
- Sockeye
- Snake tongue
- Stabbing
- Strawberry
- Sumac
- Sunburn
- Sunset
- Tomato
- Tongue
- Tuberose
- Turkey
- Venetian
- Vermillion
- Watermelon
- Wound

WHITE

WHITE is the color of innocence, goodness, purity and cleanliness. It is for weddings and medical uniforms, heroes and heavenly beings. It can also mean surrender, mourning or blankness.

Phrases: white knight, white as snow, white sale, white elephant, white list, whitewash, white lightning, white knuckle, whiteout, white light, white hat, white as a sheet, white lie, lily white, white wash, white collar, whiter than white, black and white, white tie, white bread, white flag, lily-livered

IVORY
IVORY is relaxing, quiet, neutral and calming. It suggests pureness yet overlays a rich, creamy warmth. Old ivory is precious.

Phrases: ivory tower, ivory dome, old ivory

WHITE

- Acadian mist
- Achromatic
- Alabaster
- Albatross
- Albino
- Albumen
- Alkali
- Alyssum
- Anemic
- Antarctic
- Antique
- Apple blossom
- Arctic
- Bloodless
- Candle wax
- Calla lily
- Cauliflower
- Chalk
- Chaste
- Cherry blossom
- Chicken thigh
- Chill out
- China
- Cloud
- Cocaine
- Coconut
- Corn silk
- Cottage
- Cotton
- Cottontail
- Cream
- Cream puff
- Creamsicle
- Crème
- Death mask
- Deathly
- Daisy
- Daisy chain
- Damask
- Devonshire cream
- Dogwood
- Dough
- Drained
- Drywall
- Eagle head
- Egg white
- Egg shell
- Egret

- Ermine
- Etiolate
- Fair
- Fang
- Fish belly
- Flour
- Foam
- Foxglove
- Freesia
- French vanilla
- Fright
- Frost
- Froth
- Full moon
- Gardenia
- Garlic
- Gauze
- Ghastly
- Ghost
- Glacier
- Golf tee
- Golf ball
- Greek temple
- Gull
- Handkerchief
- Hoary
- Ice
- Ice age
- Ice cream
- Ice cube
- Iceberg
- Icing sugar
- Immaculate
- Iridescent
- Irish linen
- Ivory
- Lace
- Lackluster
- Lamb
- Lamb's wool
- Lather
- Latte
- Lighthouse
- Lightning
- Lily
- Lily of the valley
- Linen
- Livid
- Marshmallow
- Mashed potato
- May apple
- Mayflower
- Meringue
- Milk
- Milkweed
- Mist
- Moby Dick
- Molar
- Moon
- Moon dust
- Moonbeam
- Moon gaze

- Moon glow
- Moonlight
- Mother-of-pearl
- Mushroom
- Muslin
- Nacre
- Napkin
- Narcissus
- Natural
- Navy
- Neutral
- North Pole
- Nougat
- Off-white
- Old lace
- Onion
- Opalene
- Opalescent
- Orchid
- Organdy
- Organza
- Oxide
- Oyster
- Pack ice
- Pale
- Pallid
- Paper
- Parchment
- Pasty
- Pearl
- Peau de soie
- Pelican
- Petticoat
- Picket fence
- Plaster
- Polar
- Polar bear
- Popcorn
- Porcelain
- Potato
- Powder
- Ptarmigan
- Puff ball
- Quartz
- Rice
- Rice paper
- Salt
- Sea foam
- Seagull
- Seashell
- Shark belly
- Shell
- Sheep
- Sheet
- Siberian
- Silvery
- Skeleton
- Ski slope
- Skull
- Skunk stripe
- Smile
- Smoke

- Snake belly
- Snow
- Snowball
- Snow bird
- Snow cone
- Snowdrop
- Snow flake
- Snow goose
- Snowman
- Snow squall
- Snow storm
- Soap suds
- Sour milk
- Spirit
- Spider web
- Splash
- Spook
- Spotless
- Stainless
- Starch
- Storm
- Suds
- Sun bleach
- Sugar
- Supernatural
- Surf
- Swan
- Swan Lake
- Tennis
- Terror

- Toad belly
- Toga
- Tooth
- Trillium
- Tundra
- Tusk
- Ultrabright
- Unblemished
- Uncolored
- Unsullied
- Untarnished
- Vampire
- Vanilla
- Virginal
- Wan
- Waterfall
- Waxen
- Wedding veil
- Wedding dress
- Wedding
- White hyacinth
- Whipped cream
- White oak
- Whiteout
- Whitewash
- Winter
- Winter solstice
- Yogurt
- Zinc

YELLOW

YELLOW is the color of sunshine. It stimulates, energized, cheers and sharpens the mind. In yellow ribbons, it signifies hope, yet it can also mean emergency, hazard, caution or cowardice. It has a high visibility.

Phrases: mellow yellow, yellow ribbon, yellow journalism, yellow streak, yellow belly, yellow peril, yellow press, yellow dog

YELLOW

- Adder tongue
- Ale
- Amaranth
- Amarillo
- Amaryllis
- Amber
- Antique gold
- Applesauce
- Aureate
- Aurulent
- Banana
- Baroque Gold
- Beer
- Bumblebee
- Butter
- Butterscotch
- Buttercup
- Canary
- Cat pee
- Cat's eye
- Chamomile
- Champagne
- Chartreuse
- Cheddar
- Cheese
- Chick
- Chicken
- Chicken liver
- Chicken leg
- Chickenshit
- Citron
- Citrus
- Corn
- Cornmeal
- Coward
- Craven

- Crocus
- Custard
- Daffodil
- Daisy eye
- Dandelion
- Dijon
- Dog pee
- Duckling
- Egg yolk
- Flaxen
- Fang
- Fire
- Flame
- Gamboge
- Gilt
- Ginger
- Gold
- Golden eagle
- Golden seal
- Goldenrod
- Goldfinch
- Grapefruit
- Gutless
- Haley's comet
- Harvest
- Honey
- Honey bee
- Honey mead
- Inca gold
- Jaundice
- Jonquil
- Larch
- Lemon
- Lemonade
- Lemon grass
- Lemonade
- Lemon ice
- Lion
- Maize
- Mango
- Margarita
- Marigold
- Marmalade
- Mayan
- Medallion
- Meteor
- Monster eye
- Morning
- Morning sun
- Mustard
- Ochre
- Old gold
- Omelette
- Panther eye
- Pernod
- Persimmon
- Pineapple
- Poltroon
- Primrose
- Quiche
- Road stripe
- Saffron

- School bus
- Slicker
- Solar
- Spun gold
- Straw
- Sulphur
- Sun
- Sun drenched
- Sun gold
- Sunbeam
- Sundance
- Sunflower
- Sunrise
- Taco chip
- Tawny
- Tiger eye
- Topaz
- Tulip
- Toucan
- Urine
- Vinegar
- Vomit
- Warbler
- Wasp
- Wheat
- Xanthic

* * * *

Boost Your Writing Even More

Now that you've seen how useful these few pages can be, imagine how a massive thesaurus of red-hot, ready-to-use marketing, fundraising or thank you phrases could supercharge your work. A real book at your fingertips whenever you need it.

This collection of colors is only **one small section** of the amazing, 495 page, Marketing Phrase Book, Professional Edition

Just imagine how much easier your work would be with such a massive, easy-to-use resource at your fingertips every day.

Perfect for Copywriters, Business Owners, Marketing and PR Pros, Web Designers, Key Word Researchers, Article Writers, Newbies and anyone else who wants to write words that sell.

Available at amazon.com **or** hamilhouse.com

Sample Entry

You not only get a lively, ready-to-use phrases, you get **valuable alternative words** plus **cross-referencing** with other entries. It's everything you need to spark your imagination, add sparkle to your writing and help you meet those deadlines.

HEART

- Sliding straight into your heart
- Let it take a place in your heart
- At the heart of things
- Bringing right into the heart of
- At the heart is
- Poured our heart and soul into it
- Young at heart
- Will always hold a special place in your heart
- Is there room in your heart for
- At the heart of this success is
- At the heart are professionals who thrive
- Open your heart and have fun
- Go with your heart
- To your heart's content
- Real people, making decisions of the heart
- Have romanced the heart for years
- Guaranteed to warm your heart
- Will warm even the coldest of hearts
- Designed to take your heart

Heart: feeling, sympathy, spirit, soul, emotion, gut feeling, sensibility, understanding, concern, kindness, goodness, love, graciousness, humanity, magnanimity, good will, bravery, daring, courage, valor, guts, fearlessness, dauntlessness, pluck, mettle, gumption, core, center, seed, kernel, substance, essence, nitty-gritty, essential

See also: **CARE, EMOTION, ESSENTIAL, FEELING, HUB, LOVE, SPIRIT**

The Marketing Phrase Book, **Professional Edition,** gives you thousands of proven-effective, ready-to-use marketing words and phrases to help you create the promotions you need to succeed. These words sell millions of dollars worth of products and services every day. Now they're at your fingertips, ready to pull in dollars for you!

Besides Colors, also included are specialized sections on The Internet, Contests, Telephone Marketing, Name that Sale, Saying No, Apology, Exclamations, Beginnings and Transitions, Reply Coupons and Power Words. Everything a marketer could possibly need to easily create top-quality, effective promotions.
ISBN 978-0-9680853-9-4, 432 pages

Order yours now*:*
amazon.com **or** hamilhouse.com

We're talking a mind-boggling, humungous, gargantuan extravaganza! Whew...even Webster would be impressed."
Entrepreneur Magazine

Also check out sister publications:

The Fundraiser's Phrase Book, Deluxe Edition

This huge resource provides thousands of positive, action-oriented phrases designed solely for the nonprofit professional. Tested, proven phrases which have **ALREADY RAISED MILLIONS OF DOLLARS SUCCESSFULLY**! Use them as building blocks for your fundraising packages, boost results, get donor dollars rolling in where they're needed most.
ISBN 978-0-9811689-0-6, 467 pages.
Available from **hamilhouse.com** or **amazon.com**

The Fundraisier's Phrase Book is building blocks that you can actually use in your letters, proposals or presentations....it goes a long way to sparking your creativity, and offers an easy escape hatch when you just can't find the right words yourself.
Canadian Fundraiser

1001 Ways to Say Thank You

We all have to say thank you every day for gifts, love, hospitality, caring help and much, much more. Sometimes, we have to apologize, sometimes convey heartfelt condolence. This very special book provides hundreds of beautiful phrases to make expressing **gratitude**, **apology** and **condolence** as easy as flicking open the pages to find exactly what you want to say. Sample letters for all occasions help you express your feelings quickly and with ease and give you fresh new words each time.

ISBN 978-0-9680853-8-7, 193 pages

Order yours now
hamilhouse.com or amazon.com

THE END